MW00834030

LISTENING TO BODIES

LISTENING TO BODIES
A Somatic Primer
for Coaches, Managers and Executives

Suzanne Zeman
Master Somatic Coach

Shasta Gardens Publishing, Richmond, CA 2008

LISTENING TO BODIES: *A Somatic Primer for Coaches, Managers and Executives.* Copyright © 2008 by Suzanne Zeman. All rights reserved. No part of this book may be used or reproduced in any manner whatsoever without written permission except in the case of brief quotations. For information address the publisher.

Shasta Gardens Publishing
1738 Shasta Street
Richmond, CA 94804

First Edition
Designed by Andrei Marcon and Suzanne Zeman

Dedicated to my teachers who taught me to observe, reflect, and design a life of purpose, passion and fulfillment. I am deeply grateful.

CONTENTS

INTRODUCTION

The body is where we experience life. It is where we live our relationships, express moods and emotions, learn, imagine the future, redeem our past, build commitments with others, protect our loved ones, and assert our dignity. Without the body there would be no possibility for tasting, hearing, smelling, feeling. There would be no thoughts, reflection, or awareness. There would be no presence to interact with itself or others, no basis for experience.

Animals rely on their senses to get information about what is dangerous, nurturing, safe, and tasty. Born with this capacity, we have intellectualized and analyzed so many aspects of our lives that we are losing the skill of paying attention to our senses. In short, we as human beings have ignored much of our animal nature, often to the detriment of our effectiveness in the world.

Learning to recover the skill of utilizing and trusting our senses provides direct access to the world around us. By increasing our awareness of sensory input, we become more effective, grounded, nurtured, and nurturing. By learning to become self-generating, we can learn to shift behaviors that we wish to change. We can improve our connection to people and find new opportunities. A rediscovery of life through our senses leads to greater satisfaction and a renewed joy in living. Ultimately, regaining the skills of feeling and sensing brings us back into more coherence and unity with the flow of life that we have cut ourselves off from. When we begin feeling, we connect with what satisfies us, what we care about, and what we want to express. For many people this comes as an awakening. It becomes possible to live a full and satisfying life, paying closer attention to our loved ones and what they care about, and finding meaningful expression through work, art, and play. These are typical results for people who develop somatic awareness. It happened for me when I began to study somatic principles and practices.

My experience of living shifted so dramatically, I decided to incorporate somatic work into the coaching I had been doing for several years with executives and entrepreneurs. Although I began studying somatics for my own healing and development, I soon recognized the power of including the body in my understanding of how people act. Working through the body along with the emotional, spiritual, and psychological aspects of a person's background provided a more complete profile for the client and for me to understand their current challenges and strengths. The results that people could achieve by increasing somatic awareness and somatic practices were dramatic.

Examples are provided in the preface: *About Somatic Business Coaching.*

Doing somatic work over the telephone began as an experiment. In my first career I was a research chemist, and created experiments to test theories and possibilities. I stayed in research, over the years switching the subject matter of my research from polymeric prototypes to studying people, how we learn, and how we can change our behaviors to be more in line with our ideal self. I was certified as an ontological[1] coach in 1992 while working in sales, marketing and business development. After several years of consulting in large-scale organizational change, design and implementation of communication strategies, the constant travel became too much, and I decided to redesign my work. After several years of study, I designed an experiment with five participants to determine whether I could help them by doing somatic work with them over the telephone. I was encouraged with the positive results, and recognized that what I was doing was innovative in the field of somatic practice. I was certified as a master somatic coach in 2001.

Other practitioners soon asked me to teach them some of the techniques and practices I use in my work, and I developed a six-session teleclass

---

[1] Ontology is the study of being. Ontological philosophy is an inquiry into the nature of human existence. In the latter part of the twentieth century, the integration of developments in the fields of philosophy and biology produced a discipline called Ontological Design by Dr. Fernando Flores. Julio Olalla and Rafael Echeverria developed the resultant coaching methodology and coaching practice, called Ontological Coaching. This discipline works with existential issues of meaning, fulfillment, happiness and worthiness in client's personal and professional lives.

For an in-depth discussion of Ontological Coaching, see *Coaching to the Human Soul: Ontological Coaching and Deep Change, Vol.I,* by Alan Seiler (Publishing Solutions Pty Ltd, 2007).

program called "Listening to Bodies Long Distance". As I continued my studies of the extended human energetic structure, I added a basic practice developed from Core Individuation™, which helps practitioners strengthen their capacity to be open, available, and aware of their own boundary to eliminate merging with difficult challenges and issues imposed by others.

When I teach these principles in person to other coaches or to my clients, the teaching and learning are very participatory. I talk about the practices, I guide the learners in the practices, answer their questions, practice again, help them if they want to go deeper, etc. In order to get the most from this primer, read the material, do the practices, reflect, journal about your observations, and repeat the practices. Repeating each practice will not only give you more confidence with the distinctions, it will also help you embody the skills for listening to your own body. Whether you are a coach, learning to do somatic work over the telephone with your clients, someone wanting to listen to your own body with greater skill and mindfulness, or an executive who wants to get more skillful in working with and relating to others, this book will give you the practices to learn.

Mastery of the practices we'll be working with requires years of repetition, so it's also helpful to be at peace with being a beginner. Recognize the competence you are developing, knowing that you have gained some skill with your own listening. With recurrence, you will be more and more competent to observe, listen, and work with others. Be patient with your learning, and have fun! Even beginners will be able to get results with the fundamental practices of body scanning, breathing and centering. You will continue to develop awareness and listening skills with every repetition – what's important is to get started and stay with each practice.

In addition to this primer, you can purchase a CD with Body Scanning and Breathing Practices from my website. The CD has helped people who are new to these practices get started.

Enjoy learning to listen to your body and the bodies of the people you work with, play with, and live with.

PREFACE: About Somatic Business Coaching

Traditional business coaching has long been recognized as a powerful catalyst for developing the skills of successful leadership. Somatic business coaching unites the power of traditional business coaching with the wisdom of somatics, or the wisdom of the entire body, mind and spirit.

The ability to mobilize and motivate others, attract talented followers, be politically astute, and think strategically are a few of the traits necessary for the consummate leader. Most business training and coaching, however, neglect the body and its enormous capacity for wisdom, energy, and leadership. Somatic coaching helps build effective leadership by using basic principles to become a fully embodied person.

When somatic intelligence and practices are incorporated into proven traditional coaching practices, powerful results can ensue. Here are some typical results achieved by incorporating somatic coaching with traditional coaching:

- *One way I used to limit success was by unconsciously maintaining a fear-based stance -- arms crossed over my chest protecting myself. Now I stand and work more professionally with my head up and arms open, ready to receive opportunities and handle challenges.*

- *Somatic coaching helped me be more centered, more grounded, more connected to spirit. I even walk differently! Rather than fall into depression, I stand my ground and walk more confidently. I am more purposeful and relaxed.*

- *My voice used to get caught in my throat when I was dealing with a difficult situation. Now I can remain calm and speak from my center. My voice is stronger, and I have seen positive reactions from my team when I speak in this new manner.*

The "body" or "soma" of somatic business coaching is very different from the mechanical body often portrayed by traditional western thinking. The traditional view emphasizes techniques, procedures and methods. It assumes there are right and wrong ways of leadership, and it often treats followers as "objects" or means for accomplishing a specific end. "Embodying" this kind of leadership requires fitting ourselves into an externally designed, pre-determined model that tells us how to dress and what attitudes to have towards others and the world.

Somatic business coaching works with each living body in its wholeness. Somatic coaches recognize that our actions are produced in our physical structure, and that our actions reflect our whole Self. This Self is the identity we have in the world, in our communities, in our organizations, in our circle of friends and in our families. It is not what we think or say about ourselves, but how we act, and how others assess these actions.

Somatics recognizes that we open or close our possibilities in the world by how we open or close our physical structures. For example, when hunched and coiled inward, I am predisposed to resignation. I limit possibilities by limiting my ability to see them and by diminishing my faith in my own resources. Not only do I overlook the resources outside myself, but I also discourage others from engaging with me.

If I wish to be open to more possibilities, I can practice feeling my feet firmly on the ground, allow my knees to be unlocked and flexible, expand my breathing and hold my head comfortably with my neck straight yet relaxed. In this stance, I am naturally more confident and more approachable. I have all "my wits about me," and I am better able to engage with others in productive relationships.

Changing, even when it is obvious what the benefits would be, is not always easy. It requires awareness and vigilance to shift our habits.

One of the most powerful somatic business coaching practices is simply to notice what is happening in the body at any given moment. "When I pay attention to body reactions," says one executive, "it's relatively easy to shift an automatic (often unconscious) reaction to an intended one. This has helped me be much more effective at work and in dialogue with my daughter - two areas I care about."

Increased personal awareness leads to increased interpersonal awareness. "Because I am more aware of my own energy and mood," says another executive, "I am also aware of the energy and mood in staff meetings and other business contexts. It's so much easier to be connected with other people at work, even people I used to consider difficult."

In many ways, somatic business coaching practices enhance traditional business wisdom. Leaders have long been expected to observe and produce ambitious moods and trust in their teams. Reading a book on trust may promote intellectual understanding, but if someone does not embody this understanding, they cannot act on it. A person may be sincere and value trust. But if their breath is high and rapid in their tight chest, if they are squeezing their eyes and freezing a smile on their face, they will have difficulty trusting, and it will be difficult for others to trust them. When they drop their breath, open their eyes, and relax, they can be authentic and be more available to others as well.

In our learning together, I will provide the basic principles that will help you increase your awareness of your body, providing access to the wisdom that will help you to live a more fully expressed and satisfying life. Doing the practices may mean making some changes, but you will be the one who decides what you want to change based on the benefits you see right from the beginning.

1. LISTENING: How do we do it?

"...too many executives think they are wonderful with people because they talk well. They don't realize that being wonderful with people means 'listening' well."

Peter Drucker[2]

We normally assume that we listen to words. A study at the University of California in 1991, however, indicated that only 7% of any communication is the choice of words; 93% is conveyed through body language and tone of voice[3]. So how do we listen to not only the 7%, but the other 93% as well? Can we and do we actually use all of our senses to listen deeply?

These are the questions I have repeatedly asked myself in the many years I have been working with people, as a body worker, Reiki practitioner, sales manager, entrepreneur, business and communications

---

[2] Drucker, Peter. *Managing the Non-Profit Organization.* Collins Publishers, 2006.
[3] Wolvin, Andrew D. *Communication Education*, Volume 40, No.2, April, 1991.

consultant, and executive coach. The conclusion I have come to is that we can educate and train ourselves to listen with full awareness, using all our senses to "hear" and interpret what others are conveying. We can all learn to do this. What's required to learn is focusing our attention on the wisdom of the body, learning to open all our senses, and being fully present in the moment with each person we are listening to. This way we can listen to the words spoken, emotions, moods, breathing, and voice of the people we interact with at work, at home, and in the marketplace. And by listening to the wisdom of our own bodies, we can interpret the full spectrum of communication that becomes available.

Why is listening important? And why do so many people complain, "no one listens around here!"? If we consider our education, most of us have not been taught how to listen. We have lots of classes on speaking, writing, and how to express ourselves and communicate clearly. But when it comes to listening, we think we already know how to do it. And if we aren't listening, all we have to do is focus on hearing what someone is saying. Hmmmm...a missing skill in almost every corporate environment, community organization, family, and relationship, and most people think they know how to do it. So why do we hear the complaint so often, "You're not listening to me!" According to a study on employee commitment, how well employees perceive that their boss listens to them affects how they view their job, *as well as their entire commitment to an organization*[4]. I want to emphasize here how important this statement is. Listening is not a nice

---

[4] Lobdell, Christine L., Sonoda, Devin T., and Arnold, William E., "The Influence of Perceived Supervisor Listening Behavior on Employee Commitment", *Journal of the International Listening Association*, Volume 7, 1993.

skill to have. It is imperative that we become good listeners if we want to be successful in today's business world.

LISTENING VALIDATES SPEAKING

We speak to be listened to. Therefore, listening validates the speaker. And when someone has the experience of not being listened to, they feel invalidated. After several attempts to "be heard", most of us stop attempting to communicate, close off the opportunity to speak, and at the most extreme, get resigned or resentful towards those who "aren't listening", or to some general authority, organization, or life as a whole.

On the positive side of the spectrum, studies indicate that simply listening with full presence validates the speaker to a point that stress and frustration can be relieved, general well-being can be improved, and relationships can be mended and re-vitalized. Therapists and doctors have reported that significant progress and healing can happen by listening deeply, even when the listener does not say or do anything else[5].

So why are we a culture of non-listeners? My premise is that we do not know how to listen. Deep listening requires using all our senses, dropping our own inner talk, staying centered and fully present to the person speaking, as though they are the most precious being to us in the moment of our conversation. This level of listening is so rare, that when it happens, we feel cherished, special, and completely validated by the person who has given us the gift of their time and attention. We

---

[5] Shafir, Rebecca Z. *The Zen of Listening: Mindful Communication in the Age of Distraction*. Quest Books, 2006.
Nichols, Michael P. *The Lost Art of Listening: How Learning to Listen Can Improve Relationships*. The Guilford Press, 1995.

can learn to listen this way to everyone we are in conversation with. It requires practice, changing habits, and a willingness to be a beginner, learning to listen with all our senses[6]. Being a good listener is easy once we learn how. Learning how means first recognizing all the ways we don't listen, accepting our habits and those patterns that prevent listening, and finally changing our habits by practicing until we have new habits that promote deep listening.

We normally assume that to listen to other people we just need to expose ourselves to what they say: be with them, talk to them, ask questions and listening will simply happen. For listening deeply, this is not enough.

The prevailing understanding of communication is based on the notion of transmission of information, developed from communication engineering (concerned with communication between machines). This framework is useful in addressing technical broadcasting issues, but is deficient when used to understand human communication.

When we deal with human communication the issue of meaning becomes critical, since we must consider how people understand what is being said. Human beings, like all living beings, are closed systems, i.e., structurally determined units. This means that what happens to us in communicative interactions is determined more by our own structure and less by the perturbing agent (i.e., the speaker). So a speaker says what he or she says, and the person "listening" not only hears the words, but more importantly, also interprets the words from their own

---

[6] Putnoi, Johanna. *Senses Wide Open: The Art and Practice of Living in Your Body.* Ulysses Press, 2000.

world of experience, history, and cultural upbringing. Environmental disturbances, i.e., things that occur from the outside, only "trigger" our responses within the range of possibilities allowed by our biology. So, for example, we don't see the colors that are out there, only the colors that our sensorial and nervous systems allow us to see. In the same way, the sounds that we can hear are determined by our biological structure. And the meanings we interpret are determined by our history, cultural environment, and upbringing.

> *"Saying does not ensure listening...the phenomenon of communication in human beings depends not on what is transmitted, but on what happens to the person who receives it".*
>
> **Humberto Maturana**[7]

Even though it is biologically rooted and rests on the phenomenon of hearing, listening is not hearing. Listening pertains to the domain of language, which includes all of our social interactions with others. What differentiates listening from hearing is the fact that when we listen we do so in a world of our own individual interpretation. Listening always implies interpretative understanding. When we ascribe an interpretation to a sound, we move from just hearing to the phenomenon of listening. We can listen when there are no sounds. Silence, gestures, body postures, and movements all can be and are interpreted.

This primer contains the practices that can teach us to be better listeners, opening our senses and awareness, and training our sensitivity. When we learn to be centered and present, we can listen to

---

[7] Maturana, Humberto R., and Varela, Francisco, J. *The Tree of Knowledge: The Biological Roots of Human Understanding.* Shambala, New Science Library, 1987.

another person with all our senses: seeing their bodies (if we are with them in person) or other images, hearing their words, feeling what their speaking and presence produces in us by noting how we feel, what we smell, and even sometimes what we taste.

Try This:

Sit comfortably with your feet on the floor, back straight, arms relaxed, shoulders relaxed, jaw dropped, muscles around your eyes relaxed, and breathing deep. Then begin noticing:

- What sounds do you hear?

- What does the air feel like? Do you feel any movement? Is it warm? Cool? Where do you feel the air?

- What aromas do you smell?

- What tastes are you tasting?

- What images do you see, either by looking externally, or closing your eyes and visualizing?

Now drop more deeply into your self.

- What sounds do you hear from inside your body?

- What do you feel? What are you aware of?

- What aromas do you smell?

- What do you taste?

- What images do you see?

Take a few moments to write down what you experienced during this exercise. The more you practice becoming aware of what all your senses are perceiving, the more deeply you will begin to listen.

When we listen with all our senses, conversations and the happenings of every day life can be amazing and transformative. As you work with each of the next chapters, opening your senses, becoming more sensitive to what you're hearing, feeling, tasting smelling and seeing, remember this possibility. And may your conversations and daily actions become even more amazing and transformative.

2. SENSATION AND BODY SCANNING

"There is no way in which to understand the world without first detecting it through the radar-net of our senses."

Diane Ackerman[8]

WHERE HAS OUR AWARENESS GONE?

The hope of our technological evolution has been to increase productivity, efficiency, and the probability of achieving more. But more of what? And to what end? Advancements in technology reduce the amount of time needed to assess, process, and deliver results at work. At the same time, workloads have increased as technological advances have helped organizations function with leaner staffing. Multi-tasking has become second nature. Global markets are easily accessible. Communicating with large audiences is not only possible; it

---

[8] Ackerman, Diane. *A Natural History of the Senses*. Peter Smith Publishers, 2002.

is more affordable than ever before. This forward movement maximizes time and consequently produces higher professional expectations for future endeavors. Yet in the face of such achievements we have to ask ourselves: Are we getting the results we expected? And what is the personal cost for such progress?

Today more than ever before, people are relying on external sources rather than on their own internal wisdom. While creating an enormous technological skill set, a social shift has also taken place as a result of humankind's progression. The expression of political, economic, spiritual, religious, and sexual ideologies transcends geographic borders. The Internet, television, best sellers, and magazines provide guidelines on what to eat, how to dress, who to love, how to live, what to drive, where to work, when to procreate, who is right, and who is wrong. This shift has changed the way information about the outside world is gathered and evaluated - affecting the mental constructs, physiology, emotional reactions, and spiritual states of many individuals. In my work as a somatic coach, I find that many people have forgotten how to access their feelings, or how to interpret sensations and information received through the body. This lack of personal awareness is a high price to pay for technological evolution.

SOMATIC AWARENESS AND THE TELEPHONE

Sensing and feeling are even more important when we are working with others. Most of us are working directly with people in our organizations, families, or through social interaction. In traditional organizations we relied heavily on visual interpretations to determine what was happening with our colleagues, managers, employees, or clients sitting face to face. However, when we're working over the telephone, the visual sense is eliminated, making it critical to develop other senses and awareness. With practice, we can increase our listening and feeling skills to notice sensations and changes in our physical, emotional, and energetic structures in response to what we hear and sense from others. Not only do we learn more about our own reactions, and ourselves, we also become more sensitive to what is happening with people and how we affect them as we work, play, love, and move around in daily life.

If you're a coach, being aware of your client's limiting behaviors and helping them act differently can be transforming for them. A coach who listens well can help a client release constraints that prevent them from acting the way they want, rather than the way they automatically react. This can be done over the telephone. It requires an ability to distinguish where constraints are located, bringing a client's attention to the specific location of the constraint or contraction, and then guiding the client's awareness to shift and release the contraction. Your ability to work through the body during telephone conversations can greatly enhance your effectiveness to help your clients increase awareness, breakthrough constraints, and become self-generating themselves.

For example, if you're leading a virtual team and speaking with a group that's located in different time zones; some may be just starting their workday while others may be ready to go home. The difference in timing alone could affect team members' ability to stay with the conversation and pay attention to important project planning. As the team leader, you'd want to be aware of people's moods, level of attention, ability to come up with solutions, recommended actions, or offers of help so you can maximize the effectiveness of your conference call.

Whether over the phone or in person, our intent as coaches is to guide clients through deep releasing and healing of patterns that are no longer useful to them. They can then be free to act in ways that will create their desired results easily, without the effort and suffering of their old behaviors. Working through the body provides information that allows us to heal, regenerate, and move more effectively in the world, relaxed and ready to respond to opportunities.

DIFFERENTATION

Managers, executives, supervisors, team leaders, consultants and coaches work directly with teams, groups, staffs, and individuals. If you are in one of these roles, can you differentiate between what you're sensing from your own internal reactions to conversations and external stimuli versus what you may be picking up from other people? Have you ever noticed that when one person in a meeting gets excited, others follow? When one begins to laugh, the humor is "catching?" Or when someone gets angry, other parties also get angry and the emotion escalates?

If you are a coach, as you begin working with a new client, it is important to determine how attuned they are to their own somatic structure and physiology. An assessment of their level of awareness will help you determine how to proceed in your work together. Additionally, it is also very important for you as a coach to be aware of your own somatic state. You need to be able to differentiate between what is happening with you and what you are picking up from your client's somatic structure and responses so you can be an objective observer and witness of the client's process.

So how do we go about learning to sense what is "ours" and what we may be picking up from someone else? Learning to increase awareness of what our senses tell us about our own personal reactions is the first step on this learning path. The Body Scan is a highly effective technique to enhance this personal awareness.

THE BODY SCAN

Body scanning is an awareness technique, focusing and bringing your attention to places where you may notice sensations, tension, or contraction. Awareness alone may bring about some change or release, promoting more energy flow, greater peace, and relaxation. The phenomenon can be explained by one of the fundamental principles of somatics: energy follows attention, i.e. where we place our attention, energy will follow.[9]

Before beginning to work with a client, listening to a colleague, or facilitating a team conversation, a body scan will tell you what your current baseline of sensation is.

Optimal Body Position

This practice may be done in a standing position, sitting, or lying down. The optimal position, especially when beginning, is standing. Here are some tips for maximizing an open posture:

---

[9] Strozzi Heckler, Richard. *The Anatomy of Change: A Way to Move Through Life's Transitions*, North Atlantic Books, 1993.

- Stand with your feet about as far apart as your shoulders or slightly wider

- Turn your toes in slightly so the outsides of your feet are parallel to each other

- Tuck your pelvis under so your spine is straight – shift around until you find the most comfortable balanced posture

- Lift gently from the crown of your head, so your spine is extended, without contracting the muscles of your back and neck

- Feel your feet flat on the floor, supporting you in a balanced and comfortable position

In this basic stance, your knees are unlocked, hip joints are open, spine is straight, and you are in a comfortable, balanced posture.

Try This:

Bring your awareness to the top of your head. Notice any sensations that are there. Do this slowly at first, giving yourself enough time to feel any sensations in your scalp and around the top of your head. Then move your awareness to your forehead and around to the back of your head. Notice any sensations that are there. Continue moving your awareness and noticing the sensations through your entire upper body, torso, legs and feet. If you find any places where you are contracted, or the muscles are tense, stay with the tension, breath, and allow the contracted muscles to relax, even if the release is slight. Pay particular attention to the following areas:

- The muscles around your eyes

- The muscles around your mouth

- Your jaw – let it drop

- Upper back, neck, and shoulders

- Upper arms, elbows, wrists, hands and fingers

- Middle back, rib cage, diaphragm and any internal organs that you can distinguish with your attention

- Lower back, belly, pelvic muscles, hips and hip joints

- Buttocks, thighs, knees, calves, ankles, feet and toes

If you feel tension, but cannot bring about a release with just your breath, you might want to try exaggerating the tension and then releasing. For example, if your upper back and shoulders feel tight, pull your shoulders up to your ears as tightly as you can, hold, hold, hold, and then with a big exhale, release completely.

When you have finished listening and practicing the Body Scan, take a few minutes to write your responses to the following questions:

- What sensations did you notice?

- What else did you become aware of?

- What did you learn?

REPETITION, EMBODIMENT, AND RESONANCE

Bringing regularity to the practice of Body Scanning will help you increase your skill level and sensitivity. Just like any new skill, it takes recurrence for the body to remember this practice. The more you practice, the easier it will be to notice sensory input, helping you interpret your environment and what's happening in your structure in response to or reaction to others. From the martial arts and adult learning studies, we know that it takes 300 repetitions for a new practice to become comfortable. It takes 3000 repetitions for a new practice to become *embodied*. Once a practice or skill is embodied, it can easily be called on as a chosen response in situations or circumstances that provoked an undesired reaction before the new skill was learned.

Embodying the practice of Body Scanning can also increase your receptivity, especially if you do the practice with this intent. Over time and recurrence, you can become sensitive to energy shifts in others and can produce a resonance in your own somatic structure that matches the state of the person you are working with. For coaches, you can develop your skill level to the extent that you can observe in your own structure what you want to bring your client's awareness to. This phenomenon is similar to the phenomenon of resonance that occurs when a vibrating tuning fork comes close to another tuning fork with identical frequency. The second tuning fork will vibrate sympathetically when in the proximity of the first vibrating tuning fork. Similarly, you can sense in your structure what another person is experiencing with their energy flow, or contraction of that flow by "tuning" to that person's somatic state. Upon reaching this state of resonance, you will find that you can coach a client to relax contractions, open areas that are constrained, and release what is ready to move, allowing them to act in ways that were not available in the contracted state. As your clients become competent observers and "scanners," they will expand their range of possibilities for generating the actions that will bring about their desired future.

FOR COACHES: SENSATION AND THE CLIENT

"To live is not merely to breathe: it is to act; it is to make use of our organs, senses, faculties—of all those parts of ourselves which give us the feeling of existence."

Jacques Rousseau

A fundamental principle in the ability to listen to bodies long distance is that energy follows awareness. Listening to the senses and learning to differentiate the sensations experienced while working with a client enables you to focus your awareness and the client's awareness to a particular area. Energy will follow this awareness and allow appropriate shifts to take place within your client's somatic structure. Let's consider why this is an important principle.

There are genetic, environmental, and historical influences that affect our somatic state on a day-to-day basis. In somatic work we work with those influences, helping our clients make shifts on a very fundamental level. Many times this will mean helping them make physical shifts in places where the muscles have contracted repeatedly in response to situations that are similar to past triggering situations, where behavior may have been learned at an early age. For example, in the last century, one of the fundamentals of parenting in some cultures included a rule that "children should be seen and not heard." Children growing up in such an environment learned to avoid being punished by not speaking around adults, not expressing their opinions, and containing themselves to win the approval of their elders. After many years of this learned behavior, the shape of the child's musculature and emotions reduces the response to speak up, thus shaping the body to contain expression. Now the child is an adult, wanting to speak up, but when the moment comes to speak, the behavior of containment is still present. By bringing the client's awareness to places where that containment occurs, they can relax the constriction, bring vitality to the musculature and learn to speak freely. First, awareness, then energy, then freedom toward new action.

The contraction or constriction of muscles in a particular part of the body will sometimes affect someone's breathing, their voice and their overall mood. So we begin with sensation to build awareness. In the next chapters, we will explore what happens when we can listen for breath, voice, mood, and the implications for effective action. By simply learning to breath you can find increased energy and a more positive emotional state. Stress decreases and contractions release. New behaviors can be learned with practice - a result of listening and paying attention to sensation.

INCREASED AWARENESS: EXECUTIVE REACTIONS

One of the most powerful somatic coaching practices is simply to notice what is happening in the body at any given moment. "When I pay attention to body reactions," says one executive, "it's relatively easy to shift an automatic (often unconscious) reaction to an intended one. This has helped me be much more effective at work and in dialogue with my daughter – two areas I care about."

Increased personal awareness leads to increased interpersonal awareness. "Because I am more aware of my own energy and mood," says another executive, "I am also aware of the energy and mood in staff meetings and other business contexts. It's so much easier to be connected and effective with other people at work, even people I used to consider difficult".

INCREASED AWARENESS: SMALL SHIFTS

At times there are very basic shifts we can make to increase the flow of energy within the somatic structure. For example, when we are sitting down the hip joints are bent. Energy flow becomes constricted by the bend. When we stand up, those channels open. I ask my clients to stand with their shoes off, keeping the outsides of their feet parallel when performing the Body Scan. This positioning of the body opens the hips, helps unlock the knees, and allows for the free flow of energy throughout the vertical channel. One client of mine, skeptical of somatic work to say the least, came to the phone with a headache, pain in her neck, and pain in her upper back. When we started the call she wasn't even aware of these pains. Within five minutes of guiding her through the Body Scan she was able to relax the muscles behind the eyes, relax her neck and eliminate all of the pain that she came to the call with. For her it was a miracle and she is no longer a skeptic. She is now practicing the Body Scan everyday.

INCREASED AWARENESS: SHIFTING INTERPRETATION

When we start developing awareness of our own sensations and discover what and to whom we react in our environment, we begin to get more control over our own reactions. We are then able to move differently. For example, two clients of mine shared a similar roadblock at work. Each client felt challenged by people in authority. Rather than speak up or voice their concerns, they got scared and didn't say anything. By practicing the Body Scan they were able to sense where their reactions began within their bodies when confronted by someone they gave authority to. Ultimately, each client was able to shift the interpretation that had them closing their mouth and not speaking their opinions or concerns. In both cases, after speaking up, they now have a much more effective working relationship with their boss. In one case, the boss thanked my client for voicing her concerns and instituted new departmental standards based on the issue she spoke up about. In the second case, my executive client felt very harshly judged, when in fact the person he reported to had a positive assessment of the executive's performance. This was only discovered when my client was able to express his opinions, ask questions, and have a more comfortable conversational exchange, which wasn't possible before increasing the executive's awareness of his constraints.

MORE PRACTICE

Do the Body Scan again. When you have finished practicing the Body Scan a second time, take a few minutes to write your responses to the following questions:

- What sensations did you notice this time?

- What else did you become aware of?

- What was different from the first Body Scan you practiced?

- What did you learn?

IN SUMMARY

Working with the body is where we as somatic coaches have the most leverage in helping our clients expand their repertoire of actions: actions that will help them achieve what they want more effectively and efficiently. Expanding this repertoire is contingent upon increasing somatic awareness. However, physiological, emotional, and spiritual awareness is only possible by connecting or in many cases reconnecting with our senses.

The Body Scan is a practice that will increase your sensitivity and awareness of your own state and your sensitivity towards the people around you. For coaches, managers and executives, this awareness will enable you to address somatic obstacles that interfere with your ability, and your clients' and employees' ability to move in ways that will bring about the fulfillment of your goals.

3. BREATHING AND BREATHING PRACTICES

"Controlled deep breathing helps the body to transform the air we breathe into energy. The stream of energized air produced by...controlled deep breathing produces a current of inner energy which radiates throughout the entire body and can be channeled to the body areas that need it the most, on demand...you can use this current of inner energy to relieve muscular tension throughout the body, revitalize a tired mind, or soothe localized aches and pains."

Nancy Zi[10]

Because of all the physiological factors affected by breathing, practices that help us breathe well also help us stay centered, calm, and therefore more effective in difficult situations.

BREATHING DEEPLY HAS MANY BENEFITS

Levels of atmospheric oxygen have steadily declined at the rate of .002 percent per year, due to pollution and climate shifts. Although this is

---

[10] Zi, Nancy. *The Art of Breathing: Six Simple Lessons to Improve Performance, Health and Well-Being.* Frog, Ltd., 2002.

not a great loss from one year to the next, the decrease has a dramatic impact on us humans over centuries. Why is the amount of oxygen we take in important?

When oxygen is in short supply (as it is for almost 90 percent of us, due to shallow breathing), the ability of intestinal villi to absorb nutrients plunges by as much as 72 percent, according to research at the University of Edinburgh in the United Kingdom. "When oxygen intake improves, nutrient absorption is enhanced within minutes, boosting metabolic rate by as much as 30 percent," says nutritionist Marc David[11]. In addition, deep breathing keeps cells oxygenated, helping the body to maintain optimal ATP (adenosine triphosphate) production, the defining factor for the conversion of food into usable energy.

There are even more benefits to breathing deeply. Up to 70 percent of toxins (preservatives, pesticides, etc.) can be converted into gases that are expelled through deep breaths, so deep breathing can remove toxicity from the body. According to studies at the Sansum-Santa Barbara Medical Foundation Clinic, simply breathing slowly and deeply to maximize the oxygen inhaled and the carbon dioxide and wastes exhaled, increases the release of fat-packing toxins by as much as fifteen fold. Research at the International Breath Institute in Boulder, Colorado shows that most people use less than 25 percent of their lungs' two-gallon capacity. When people improve their breathing and maximize their oxygen intake, they can more than double the amount of body fat they oxidize and burn each week.

---

[11] David, Marc. *The Slow Down Diet*. Healing Arts Press, 2005.

Keeping the bloodstream oxygenated calms the entire central nervous system, lowering production of the stress hormone cortisol by as much as 50 percent in 10 minutes. When oxygen levels are high and the nervous system is calm, the pancreas responds by reducing its production of fat-storing insulin. So breathing deeply can help with weight loss and increasing available energy!

DISTINCT WAYS TO BREATHE

Just about everyone is conscious of, or easily recognizes the inhalation and exhalation of breath. This includes people who haven't developed any awareness of their own body or feelings. They know that they're breathing and most can identify where in their body they feel their breath. Once they can feel their inhalation and exhalation, I ask them, "Where is your breath actually located right now?"

For the purposes of practicing, I make a distinction between four distinct ways of breathing. There are many breathing practices in yogic and eastern traditions, however, being able to distinguish and practice these four, will provide you with foundational practices for yourself and the people you are working with. I call these distinct ways of breathing: high, middle, dropped and full torso breathing.

When I refer to **high** breath, I am highlighting the breathing that happens mostly in the upper chest - also known as shallow breathing. When breathing in the upper chest we are not using the expansion of the torso to fill our lungs. Rather, to get the oxygen we need to function, we breathe faster.

Middle breathing or mid-torso breathing, on the other hand, takes in more air with each inhale, due to the expansion of the ribcage while inhaling. You can feel the expansion of the ribs by placing your hands on the sides of your rib cage and allowing your hands to move outward as you inhale - allowing them to move in as you exhale.

The third breath I refer to is a **dropped** breath. Dropped breath uses more of the volume of the lungs. In this case, it's the belly that is expanding while inhaling and contracting while exhaling, filling the lungs from the bottom, where the largest capacity is. In dropped breathing, the ribs are moving but the upper chest remains relatively still. Most of the movement is low in the torso. Breathing from the belly uses more lung capacity and also increases blood oxygenation - building greater stamina and immediately increasing available energy.

By optimizing the use of our lungs, which thereby optimizes oxygenation and energy availability, we can bring the three distinct ways of breathing together - using the entire torso in **full torso** breathing. Full torso breathing starts in your belly, expanding your ribs as you inhale and continues as you bring your breath softly into your upper chest, followed by a complete exhalation before breathing in again.

FOR COACHES

Remember when you are working with a client to check in with them by asking where they are breathing. This will help you determine their awareness, and will also validate what you are sensing in your own structure as you listen.

For example, at times I will start to feel anxious while listening to a client talk about their work situation, difficult conversations they are worried about, or some other challenge they are facing. Sometimes I can feel their anxiety in their greeting. My own sensations are a sign for me to ask where they are breathing. Most likely, their breath is located up high in their chest, increasing their tension, causing the pace of their breath to be faster than when it's dropped.

Once they can feel their breath, we can go on to determine whether breathing this way is helping them take the actions they are wanting to take, or hindering them to be the way they want to be and be perceived by others. So the breath alone can optimize their readiness for certain actions, and minimize options for other actions.

HIGH LEVEL BREATHING: WHAT IS IT GOOD FOR?

It's important to realize that each type of breathing opens and closes possibilities. We are often told that the best way to breath is in your belly. I agree with that for the most part, however in many corporate environments, where people are "in their heads," moving at a very fast pace, using their mental facilities without feeling the senses – high breathing can be helpful to "fit in", connect, and then choose whether we want to remain breathing that way.

To connect with colleagues who are breathing fast and high, be perceived as credible by them, and fit into the culture, it can help to bring your breath up higher in your chest. This kind of breathing is useful for analytical thinking, data analysis, and other tasks that require a narrow focus. You can do this and remain grounded and centered, if you are somatically aware and present in your body. In most corporate environments today, we see people walking around, lost in thought, breathing high. Their whole structure is kind of narrow and contracted. You will also notice that when they move, they are leaning forward, leading with their head. Another way to help someone counteract this automatic way of moving is with a practice I call "heel down walking".

Try This:

Imagine that your lungs are only functioning in the upper part of your chest. Draw your breath up, inhaling by expanding the very top of your chest, and exhale as best you can by releasing the chest muscles. If you can isolate your breathing into the upper chest completely, you may also notice the pace of your breathing increasing. This is because you will have to breathe faster to get more oxygen into your lungs and bloodstream. Reflect for a moment, and write down your responses to the following questions.

- What does this level of breathing produce for you?

- What are you noticing about your attention?

- Your awareness of your surroundings?

- Your awareness of people?

- How does the external world appear?

- What's possible?

- What's not possible?

Practice: Heel Down Walking

This practice is an antidote for people who are walking fast, breathing fast, leaning forward, leading with their head. This way of moving around makes it difficult to be aware of others, and often leads to an assessment that the person is distracted and unavailable.

The practice of walking by placing the heel of the foot down on the ground first and rolling onto the whole foot will help the person's body shift back to a more vertical line, instead of leading with the head. This automatically helps slow the pace of the walk, and allows an easier dropped breath. Many of my clients have found this practice beneficial; especially if they are working on making stronger connections with their colleagues and people they are managing. Slowing the pace of their breathing and walking allows their vision to include others, opening their peripheral vision to take in a broader expanse of the environment. This produces an assessment that the person is open, ready to engage, and is seeing the bigger picture.

MID-LEVEL BREATHING: CONNECTING WITH OTHERS

Mid-level breathing facilitates opening awareness to include others, as when working with a team, facilitating a group process, or when you want to connect with a community. You can stay active and focused, for example, on the purpose and agenda of a meeting, drop your breath and connect with the entire group of people you are facilitating by breathing in the middle of your torso. Breathe by expanding your ribs - extending your energy out through your sides (in the horizontal direction), and then connect to and hold the group with your awareness. This may seem complicated at first, but with practice breathing in this way will ease the extension of energy in the horizontal direction (opening your energetic **width**). Your breath can come up a little from your belly but notice when you breathe out from your sides how much easier it is for your energy to follow. You'll find that developing your breathing in the horizontal direction can help you expand to connect and extend to a group easily.

Practice mid-level breathing by moving your ribs out as you inhale. Extend your energy horizontally, lifting your arms as though opening to and holding a giant beach ball. Notice what happens. You may begin to feel larger, more expansive, and more relaxed with yourself and the people you are with. If you feel unsettled or "spacey", extend your energy down into the earth through your legs and feet, planting yourself firmly on the ground.

Try This:

Place your hands on your ribs on the sides of your torso, and let your ribs push your hands out as you inhale, feeling your ribs dropping in as you exhale. Continue practicing this mid-level breathing, taking several deep breaths using your ribs to control your breath.

- Where does your awareness naturally open?

- What happens as you extend your width?

- Where do you experience more freedom?

- What holding or contraction do you notice?

- What happens as you continue breathing this way?

- What questions does your mind open to?

- How do people appear when you breathe this way?

DROPPED BREATH: SETTLING DEEPLY INTO YOURSELF

Isolating your breathing in the bottom of your torso can help open the lower portion of your structure. This allows for a greater flow of energy to your legs, feet, and ultimately to your connection with the earth. Energetically connecting to earth or ground is often called "being grounded." This connection is important when you want to establish credibility as an authority or expert with content, or delivering a communication that means something to you, when you are facing conflict, or some potential danger. When you bring your breath down, your attention and energy can easily move down as well. You can move more easily from your center, extending as needed, open to meet whatever or whoever is coming toward you with confidence and stability - rather than contraction and fear. This is helpful, for example, when you are preparing for a difficult conversation, preparing to work with a client who has challenging issues to work with, or any situation that is new, unfamiliar, or threatening.

Practicing to isolate your breathing by using your belly helps train your muscles. With recurrence, you'll find that during times of stress or challenge, your breathing can easily shift to provide support for your intent in the situation.

Try This:

Place one or both hands on your belly, just below your belly button. Take a few breaths to feel the expansion and contraction of your belly as you inhale and exhale. Make sure your hand(s) are being moved in and out with your belly – extending out as you inhale, and dropping as you exhale.

- Where does your attention go as you practice?

- What becomes more available?

- What becomes less available?

- What happens to your shoulders, chest and neck as you continue this dropped breathing?

- What about your thoughts?

You can practice isolating your breath even further with this "belly breathing" (for the sake of increasing your mastery) by keeping almost all of the movement in the lowest part of your torso – relaxing the mid-section, chest and shoulders fully. This helps your mid and upper body stay relaxed and ready to respond to whatever is coming your way – movement, conversations, circumstances – with full awareness, choosing the best action in the moment.

Try This:

First exhale completely. Now, begin inhaling by expanding your belly, drawing your breath softly upward slightly, while keeping most of the movement around your pelvis and lower torso. As you continue breathing this way, allow your chest, shoulders and neck to relax each time you exhale, increasing the relaxation of those areas until any tension has dissipated completely.

- What do you notice now?

- Continue breathing this way and bring your awareness to your pelvis, hips, thighs, knees, calves, ankles, and feet, extending energetic roots down through your feet into the earth.

- What do you notice as you connect into the earth, grounding yourself this way?

FULL TORSO BREATHING: INTEGRATING AND FULLY EXPRESSING

When all three of the above ways of breathing are integrated, you can breathe using your full torso. You are then maximizing oxygen intake and facilitating the exchange of gases through the tissues of the lungs and bloodstream, supporting and nourishing all physical processes and maximizing stamina. Full torso breathing also facilitates extending energy in all directions, optimizing length, width, and depth of the somatic and energetic structure

Try This:

Begin your breath way down in your torso by expanding your belly to inhale. Continue inhaling, opening your ribs, feeling your breath move up into the middle of your torso. As you draw your breath on up into your chest, see if you can keep the muscles of your upper chest, shoulders and neck relaxed and open. It may help to release any tension you notice every time you exhale. Continue breathing this way for several rounds.

- What are you noticing?

- What happens when you extend your energy vertically, opening more length?

- Horizontally, opening more width? Back to front, opening greater depth?

When our somatic and energetic structure are open and extended, we are fully available, relaxed and ready to meet whatever comes our way with our full faculties prepared to respond. So not only is this the optimal way for us to breathe in preparation for working with our clients, but we can also help our clients by introducing this way of breathing into their program of practices.

4. VOICE NOTES

Although interpreting the human voice is one of our most important daily social activities, the way we speak and hear remains almost entirely hidden, and unexplored. Those who develop a richer understanding of the voice are less likely to mishear their friends, lovers, rivals, and more able to intuit when people are being authentic or dishonest.

Anne Karpf[12]

What is your voice saying about you? What happens when people hear your voice? Is your voice strained, constricted, or tense? Or is it relaxed, full, and resonant? These are questions you'll be considering and working with in this chapter.

---

[12] Karpf, Anne. *The Human Voice: How This Extraordinary Instrument Reveals Essential Clues About Who We Are.* Bloomsbury Publishing, 2006.

IDENTITY

Identity can mean how we see ourselves as individuals and how we define ourselves, or it can mean the phenomenon of how we are known or seen by others, often different from the way we see ourselves. For the sake of coherence, the gap between how we know ourselves and how others see us becomes important. The smaller the gap, the stronger the coherence. Voice then becomes an important factor in how we appear to others, either in person or on the telephone.

The physical voice, the sound produced by the vocal cords (or folds) and resonated by the cavities of the head, throat and torso, conveys qualities that a listener interprets. For example, if someone's voice sounds sharp or piercing, the speaker may be seen as curt, unapproachable, angry, or mean. Conversely, someone who has a melodic, pleasant voice may be seen as friendly, approachable, or nice to be around. Think about what your voice says about you, and how others are impacted when they hear your voice.

Voice can also have a broader, metaphorical meaning. Clients have come to me asking for help to "find my voice". What does this mean? Usually, it means that a person wants to be able to speak what is real and authentic for them. So not only would we be working on the words they're saying, the meaning they're conveying, and the melody of the sounds, but also looking deeper into the person they are becoming and how they want to express what they are discovering that has value for them. Voice is the carrier of that expression.

When you want to speak about what is meaningful and important to you, you'll want your voice to be able to express that meaning in a way the your listeners can hear the depth and importance of your message. The quality of your voice can convey what you want, or the quality can convey an entirely different characteristic.

QUALITY

"No other human activity is more influenced by breathing than vocalization."

Nancy Zi[13]

How we are breathing directly affects the quality of our voice. Experiment with this yourself. Bring your voice all the way up into your upper chest, breathing so that your throat is slightly constricted, and then say your name out loud. You might also try reading a few sentences out loud to have more words to speak and feel.

Now drop your breath to the level of your ribs (mid level breathing), relax your throat, and as you speak, feel the vibration of your voice in the upper part of your torso. What does this voice feel like? What does it convey?

And drop your breath all the way to your belly, relaxing your torso and diaphragm so your voice resonates all the way into your torso. As you say your name now, how does it sound to you? Ask a friend or colleague what happens when they hear your voice in these different ways. What does it produce for them? And which voice is most coherent with the identity you want to produce in different situations?

---

[13] Zi, Nancy. *The Art of Breathing: Six Simple Lessons to Improve Performance, Health and Well-Being.* Frog, Ltd., 2002.

As a professional? With your friends? With your family? In front of an audience?

CHOICE

I can remember one day when I was high school age answering the phone. It was my father's boss. After the call, Dad said his boss asked the age of his little daughter. I was offended, but realized at that point that my high pitched voice was not sounding like the grown up woman I wanted to be seen as. In addition, when I went to college, my councilor recommended that I take a speech class to rid myself of the New Jersey accent that betrayed my origins. That was the last straw. I committed to retraining my voice. I listened to tapes, practiced breathing techniques, and even took some singing lessons. After a year, the quality of my normal speaking voice changed. I no longer had a regional accent, and did not sound like a child.

In addition, the practices I did had other benefits that surprised me. My friends started asking me to help them think about challenging situations, I was sought out for advice, and generally being taken more seriously. I could still laugh out loud and giggle like a kid when having fun, so that didn't change. However, my range of expression was expanding. I was learning how to use my voice as an instrument of deeper expression.

In his book, The Heart Aroused: Poetry and the Preservation of the Soul in Corporate America David Whyte wrote a chapter called "Fire In the Voice". Here is one of my favorite excerpts from that chapter:

"The voice, after all, is entering the body of the listener and radically affecting his inner world. A word...is focused by the outer funnel of the ear, gathered on the membrane of the eardrum, and passed through a watchmaker's arrangement of three tiny bones to the salty fluid of the inner ear. This minuscule inner sea responds to sound the way the real sea responds to the moon, shifting with tidal currents hundreds of tiny hairs rooted in the auditory nerve cells. The emotional and imaginal world radiates out from those ear follicles through the whole length of the body on a tide of electrical impulses, warming the heart, sickening the stomach, or stimulating the adrenals in an instant to fight or flight."[14]

IMPACT

How is your voice impacting the bodies that it touches? Does it warm the heart or sicken the stomach? How would you even know?

Try recording your voice and listen to how you sound. How do you describe the voice you've recorded? Is this your "normal" voice? Were you nervous during the recording? What effect did your anxiety produce?

Try This:

Experiment with breathing. Drop your breath, relax your throat and the upper part of your torso, and record your voice again. Listen, reflect, and write down your observations. What do you notice this time?

Describe how your voice sounds when you're angry. Or tense. Or rushed. Or sad. Or happy!

If you're not sure, imagine yourself in a situation where you were angry, and record your voice. Do the same for other moments where

---

[14] Whyte, David. *The Heart Aroused: Poetry and the Preservation of the Soul in Corporate America.* Doubleday, 1994

you were tense, hurrying, sad, happy, etc. Take a few notes after reflecting and describe your observations.

Which voice is how you want to be heard? Which voice is friendliest? Most melodic? Inviting? What practices will help you have the voice that produces the identity you want to be known for?

FOR COACHES

All of the practices I've described are tools for coaching. Whether in person or on the telephone, your client's voice reveals their current emotional state, and can also indicate the prevalent mood that is the background for their world view. As you listen to their description of their circumstances, what melody comes to the forefront? Is it lilting and happy? Monotone and strained?

Listen to the voices you hear, not only from your clients, but also on the radio and television. Identify what you can distinguish from each person's voice. What can you tell about their breathing from their voice? Is what you're hearing consistent with the person they are, or the character they are conveying?

What practices can you ask your clients to do that will help them have a full and expressive voice? What practices will help them soften their voice, not decreasing the volume, but making it easier to be listened to? What practices will produce a deeper, more grounded, and stronger voice?

In the next two chapters we will be working with mood and centering. As you learn more about these topics, remember to bring your observations and what you're learning about voice to understand how they can impact your work and expand your repertoire of tools and practices.

5. LISTENING TO BODIES IN FOUR BASIC MOODS

"No matter where we are and no matter what we are doing, we human beings are always in a mood. Ordinarily we don't choose or control our moods – we just find ourselves in them. Once in a particular mood, we become what that mood allows us to be."

Rafael Echeverria[15]

Moods are fundamental to human beings. We live in moods. Certain actions are available or not available to us when we're in particular moods. Our bodies both determine what moods we are in and what moods are available to us, and our moods can also determine how our bodies are shaped. In that way, moods are a physical presentation of our assessments and opinions.

When I say, "I feel great today!" I will most likely be standing tall, in an open posture, seeing a broad vista, and ready to act on opportunities

---

[15] Echeverria, Rafael. "On Moods and Emotions," *Mastering the Art of Professional Coaching,* private publication, 1991.

that come my way. On the other hand, when I say to myself or to a colleague, "This company stinks, it's never going to change, and I'm not appreciated for all the hard work I've put in," my body will most likely be slumped over, collapsed, I'm looking down, and not much is possible. Imagine being slumped over, sitting at your desk and saying "I feel great today!!" The shape of a bent over, collapsed body doesn't match a mood of feeling great. Similarly, imagine standing tall with arms outstretched to the sky saying, "This company stinks, it's never going to change, and I'm not appreciated for all the hard work I've put in." The shape and the speaking are not coherent. So moods and the shapes of bodies in those moods predispose us to certain ways of thinking, speaking, and acting.

In addition, our opinions often become habitual thoughts that lead to automatic interpretations, coloring how we view the world. So our moods directly affect our capacity to take action and coordinate effectively with others. And our moods directly affect the quality of our relationships since people respond to our moods. This is an important principle in somatic work, because the mood we are in can determine how well or how poorly we connect with and listen to others, their concerns, their feedback, and their motivations.

As we become more competent in seeing and listening to somatic shapes with the distinctions of sensation, breathing, and voice, we can hear what mood people are in. We do this by listening to the stories and interpretations they express, sensing their somatic shape from the way our own body responds, whether in person or via telephone. A person's somatic shape tells us where they are contracted or constricted, and how open and available they are.

MOODS SHOW OUR ORIENTATION TO THE FUTURE

Why am I giving importance to the phenomenon of moods, and listening for a person's mood? I'm interpreting mood as the background thinking and view of life that predisposes what actions are possible or not possible for someone. Another way to say this is that moods reflect a person's orientation to the future. This is different from emotions, which are triggered by some event and are short-lived (such as sadness over a loss or happiness over some good fortune). Moods, on the other hand, last for long periods of time, even a lifetime, or over generations (as in families, societies, or cultures).

For example, if someone is deeply resigned, the conversation that they are living in that's in the background, defining how they see the world, is something like, "Nothing I can do will change anything." That conversation affects what they see possible, or not. If they are resigned, they see nothing possible, and any attempt to show something new will fall into the old interpretation. For coaches, if coaching is going to be successful, the person's mood must be addressed. Working with the background conversations and interpretations can change moods; however, working through the body is often deeper and more effective. Moods are embodied, so even when working with the conversations the person is living in, the body will eventually shift as well. With effective practices, moods can be permanently altered.

Each mood has a body shaped to be an expression of that mood. Following our example, then, what is the body of someone who is resigned? Imagine yourself thinking, "Nothing I do will change anything around here. It's all hopeless anyway. I don't know why I even try."

What happens to your body? Most people who live in the story of resignation have their head down, they sit and stand slumped over, and their walk is slow and shuffling.

What's the body of someone who is resentful? Try saying over and over, "Those people (or that person) have determined my fate and are to blame for my miserable condition." Or, "S(he) has done me wrong and it's her/his fault that my life is the way it is." With resentment, there is also a commitment **not** to talk to the person(s) that we are blaming, but to silently continue to blame them for whatever they did to make us miserable. There is an anger and hostility that is internalized – what is this shape? Imagine a body that has arms crossed, protecting and closing off any possibility of connection or intimacy, narrow or squinted eyes, slumped down with no commitment to take action to resolve their own misery.

On the positive side, there is a body of acceptance, which produces a mood of peace. The conversation may be, "Possibilities may or may not be closed to me here, and I am still grateful for what life brings." Or, "I'm willing to accept the way things are at the moment and deal with what is." This body is open, at peace, calm and centered. From here, new actions can be designed, or the person may settle into the current situation without complaint, open to what will unfold.

When we have an acceptance of current conditions, and motivation to change our circumstances, bring a new project or enterprise into existence, or invent a new strategy, we are in a mood of ambition. The background conversation may be, "Wow! There's a future for me here, and I'm going to make it happen!" What's the shape of the body that is coherent with this background? When we are in this mood, we are open, often even smiling, enjoying life and engaging with people, the voice has a lilt to it, we are breathing freely, energy is flowing and there's an easy vitality that is attractive to people around us.

The following chart provides a quick overview of these 4 basic moods:

	We Cannot Change Circumstances	We Can Change Circumstances
Moods of Denial	**RESENTMENT**	**RESIGNATION**
Moods of Acceptance:	**PEACE**	**AMBITION**

Adapted from the writings and teachings of Dr. Fernando Flores and Dr. Rafael Echeverria.

There are many variations of these moods, and each has a particular background conversation that and body shape that produces the mood.

Try This:

The following expressions, whether spoken or not, can help you to recognize the background thinking of each mood. See what happens to your body as you "try on" each expression. Repeat the expression several times until your body takes on the mood. Then pay attention to the shape that you find yourself in.

POSITIVE MOODS

ambition   There are future possibilities for me here and I am committed to take action to make them happen.

serenity   Possibilities may be opened or closed for me at any time, and I am grateful to life.

trust   Based on your past record (performance and actions), I assess that you will fulfill your promises to me.

acceptance   Possibilities may be closed for me here and I am still grateful to life.

wonder   I don't know what is going on here. I see possibilities for myself, and I like it!

resolution   I see possibilities here and I am going to take action right now.

confidence   I am competent to act in this domain and I have evidence to show you why I say so.

NEGATIVE MOODS

resignation   Nothing is going to get better here. It has always been and it will always be this way. And there is nothing I can do about it.

despair   I see immediate negative possibilities for myself here. No one, no matter who, can take action to change this.

distrust   You never have and never will fulfill your promises to me or anyone else.

resentment   You have closed possibilities for me. I hold you responsible for this, and I am committed to not having a conversation with you about this.

confusion   I don't see what is going on here. I don't know what to do next, and I don't like it.

panic   Future possibilities will be closed for me if I do not work harder and faster right now!

arrogance   I claim that I already know and my assessments are true. There is nothing else you can add here, and you should listen to me.

Enjoy practicing with these various moods and the conversations that provoke them. See what shape the bodies are that live in these moods. Not only does one's mood predispose what actions may or may not be possible; a person's mood greatly affects their identity and ability to provide leadership. Would you be more inclined to follow someone who is in a positive and accepting mood, or someone who is resigned or resentful?

FOR COACHES

Most people look for coaches who can help them make some change or shift in their way of seeing the world, so they can achieve an outcome different from where they find themselves. From a coaching perspective, once you have recognized the mood someone is in, how can you help them change their mood? The key principles to work with are the shape of the body and the story the person is telling about their situation or their life.

When someone tells you their story, you can listen for not only the circumstances, but also the background that led to the conclusions and assessments a person is making, the history of actions that got them to where they are, and the melody of the telling. The melody comes from the body – so even if you are working over the phone, you'll be able to listen for much of what determines a person's mood. Once a mood is identified, what then? The more you can help a person become aware of the shape of their body in a particular mood, the easier it will be to provide practices to help them shift that shape. For example, you might ask, "Where are you breathing right now? How are you sitting, or standing? Describe your posture to me. What does that breathing or posture produce for you? What happens if you drop your breath (for example)? What do you notice? What happens if you stand taller and relax your shoulders (another example)? What do you notice then?

With this line of questioning, you are increasing the person's ability to observe themselves. Once you've identified together the "old" body and the "new" body, you can design practices to help them remember the new body. With practice, the new body will become more authentic, and the story will also change. Shifting the story can also be accelerated with journaling, or ongoing practice of telling a new story about a situation in a way that's authentic.

For example, I was in a mood of resentment for years about the work I was doing. No matter what I did, it was not enough for me to be satisfied. As a research chemist, I enjoyed working in the laboratory, but I wanted to be working with people. In business, I had other complaints, or dissatisfactions. After a string of starting different career paths, I started thinking about what happened at home while I was growing up. I remembered that we always waited for my Dad to come home, and then we sat down at the dinner table. Then Dad talked about his day. All we heard were complaints. My Dad supervised a warehouse crew, and we heard all the stories about how lazy this one was, how slow another one was, how the boss was pressuring him to get them to be more efficient, etc. etc. etc. He never spoke about himself, only about how wrong everyone else was, and how miserable it made him. It sounded like my liturgy when I came home! I began to see how the resentment about work became part of my heritage and embodiment.

To begin to change my view, I started journaling at the end of every workday, asking myself the questions, "What am I grateful for today? Who did something that I appreciated? Did I acknowledge the people working with me?" And similar questions to keep my thoughts focused in a positive direction. Prior to journaling, I did some deep breathing and centering practices. I did these practices for a year, focusing on my mood. At the end of that time, I was working joyfully, looking forward to my work every day. My stories at the end of the day were very different as well. And then I redesigned my work to be what I now see as the fulfillment of my purpose. It's the work I'm still doing today, and loving every day of it.

6. BASIC PRACTICES: Centering, Length, Width, and Depth

"Center is a living process of self-organization that increases our capacity to be self-generating, self-healing, and self-educating. To center ourselves is to shape ourselves in a particular way to life. It is a pattern of organization that expresses the self we are at any given moment. Center is a state of unity in which effective action, emotional balance, mental alertness, and spiritual vision are in harmonious balance. When we're centered, our actions are coherent with what we care about."

Richard Strozzi Heckler[16]

Ideally, our practices are those activities that shape us to be able to perform at our best. When we're not fully aware of our bodies, or our mental and emotional states, the practices that we do are simply habits, either helping us be more effective, or producing greater states of unconsciousness. Even though we're always practicing *something,* we're usually not aware of what we're practicing, or what our habitual

---

[16] Strozzi Heckler, Richard. *Holding the Center: Sanctuary in a Time of Confusion.* Frog, Ltd., 1997.

practices produce for us. The basic practices that are described here can produce more openness, awareness, and greatly increase our ability to take effective action.

How do these practices help? When our minds scan for problems and recall past problems in an effort to ensure that we don't repeat them, we often get caught in an endless loop: replaying, replaying, replaying, replaying. These loops could direct us to make the future look exactly like the past because the past is a known quantity and it's safe and predictable. Awareness of this automated process is the first step in getting free from its clutches.

Try This:

To quickly move out of "auto mode" and put your thinking into "manual mode", use the following centering practice. Centering is a simple, powerful exercise that increases your ability to focus right now. Read this through and then stop for a moment:

- Take a deep breath starting in your belly, using the full torso breathing described in the paper "Breathing and Breathing Practices".

- Pay attention only to your breath for those few seconds.

- Keep breathing into the "center" of your body . . . three breaths, five.

- Bring your focus back to the task at hand and notice the subtle shift in your ability to direct your focus.

Take a few moments to reflect on what you experienced as you did this practice, and write down your observations. The more often you practice, the better able you will be to direct and focus your attention. By centering a few times a day, you build your ability to focus at will, for longer and longer periods of time.

Your physical **center** is a few fingers below your belly button – a place to drop your attention to when you feel anxious, or don't know how to move in a situation. You can tap your belly to help shift your attention quickly, bringing you to an openness and greater willingness to see what is happening without the distraction of your automatic ideas and opinions. Center is a bodily and energetic "base camp" that can be used as a way to focus, learn, and move through transitions. It helps you to feel bodily present to yourself and your situation. The state of center is a doorway to begin feeling your possibilities in the world, not as a rigid quality, but as a state to help you develop and access other parts of yourself. The power of center is in assisting you when you feel lost, anxious, or uncertain.

From center, you can then tune in to the flow of energy through you, and open those places where you are constricting your breathing and energy flow.

LENGTH

Length is the energetic dimension to practice when you want to connect your actions to what you care about, build a strong ground or foundation, or any situation where a strong grounded presence is required. When you find yourself mindlessly repeating tasks, or overwhelmed by the details of everyday living, practice developing your length, and remember what you care about.

Try This:

Scan through your body from top to bottom, feeling your vertical line – your **length**. By opening to the flow of energy through you, you can touch the core of the earth, bringing yourself to a deeper connection with ground, while opening to spirit through the crown of your head. When connected through your vertical line, you are the channel for bringing spirit to earth, and earth to spirit. Take a few moments to reflect on your experience, and write your responses to these questions:

- What did you feel when you connected to ground/the earth?

- What did you notice as you connected to spirit by "opening" your crown?

- What happens when you are open to spirit and earth simultaneously?

Imagining your energetic roots reaching down into the earth from your feet, and dropping your energetic tail down from the end of your spine can develop length. These are the natural connecting points from our physical bodies to the ground. Establishing these connections provides a "grounded" presence. This is helpful when we want to establish authority, take a stand for something important to us, or simply feel our inherent strength.

Repeat the practice of extending your length, and remember to write down your observations and experiences as you practice to reveal and acknowledge what you are learning.

WIDTH

The dimension of **width** is the social dimension. By opening yourself in the horizontal plane, you can experience confidence in your capacity to hold more commitments, connect more easily with a community, and feel your place in social environments.

Try This:

To open your width, bring your breath to the mid-torso level, feeling your ribs expand and relax as you inhale and exhale. Then extend your energy in the horizontal direction, by expanding energetically through the sides of your structure. You may want to open and lift your arms, as though holding a giant ball – this can help you open your energetic width to become a more open container for all that you're holding. Let yourself open to this dimension when you feel overwhelmed, alone and despondent, or when you want to securely hold all the commitments you have made to the people you care about. Continue practicing opening the dimension of width, and note your responses to the following:

- What do you experience as you "get wider"?

- How do other people appear when you open this dimension?

- How do you experience your capacity as you widen your structure?

This is a practice you will find helpful during transitions, when you are starting a new project, when you are working in a new environment, or when you are joining a new community. In addition to helping us find a place of comfort within ourselves, opening width also can help us have compassion for our humanness and comfort with being a beginner in any new territory.

DEPTH

The dimension of **depth** gives us the momentum to move forward in life, maintaining awareness of all that is behind us, backing us up. What "backs us up" includes our history and all of our life experience.

Try This:

To practice opening your depth, begin with full torso breathing, and bring your attention to your back. As you breathe, extend your energy behind you, and at the same time bring to mind all of your history: your life experience, all that you've learned, the people who have supported you, your teachers, colleagues, friends, family, mentors, ancestors, and spiritual guides. Continue opening and extending back until you feel comfortable with that expansion, you have a strong experience of your history, and feel the confidence of being supported by the past. Then take all that energy forward through your torso, and extend out in front of you, all the way forward, reaching to the horizon. Continuing to expand the energy you extended from your back and moving it forward can increase the dimension of depth. Continue practicing and write down what you observe in response to these questions:

- How far back can you extend your energy? If you don't feel anything, or cannot extend beyond your skin, lean up against a tree and feel the life force in the tree through your back. Extend into that life force. Then slowly move away, while maintaining the connection. With practice and increasing sensitivity, you will be able to extend your energy back without the tree or other living energetic body to connect to. You can also practice connecting through your back to another person by standing back to back, connecting, and very gradually moving apart, still feeling the connection energetically.

- What happens as you open to your history and all the life experience that supports you in moving forward to your future?

- How confident do you feel after doing this practice several times?

Go forward with confidence and competence, leading others toward the vision that you can hold by maintaining your vertical line and connection to what's important, while moving your energy out from your back, through your center to the horizon in front of you.

FOR COACHES

Paying attention to the dimensions of length, width, and depth can help you locate how to help your clients with their learning challenges by connecting their somatic practices to what they are learning. Start by guiding them with a centering practice, then assess their ability to open to each dimension, noting especially where they are challenged and how their somatic challenges connect to what they are working on. By focusing on somatic practices, you can help them move and present themselves in ways more consistent with the future they are designing.

SUMMARY

These fundamental practices will help you feel life as a tangible experience, and your body awareness can then be used as a doorway to the realms of intuition, perception, and expression. These are not ends in themselves, but can help you move to a strong connection into yourself to carry into your dialogues with others, your work, and the deeper aspects of who you are as leaders in your families, businesses, communities and the world.

Remember, we are always practicing something. So choose your practices to help you be the person you want to be!

7. GETTING BIG: Practices to Expand to the Edge

Any time merging with another occurs, or it is impossible to resist being pulled into the story or scenario of another person, it is safe to say your awareness is not at the Edge. Losing the ability to see, to feel, or to know yourself as separate and distinct from another person, is off base. In these situations: stop, assess, and begin again to reach the Edge.

Desda Zuckerman[17]

Imagine a moment that happened recently, when you felt stressed, pressured, emotional, or otherwise impacted by circumstances outside your control. Remember how you felt? Wouldn't it be great to have ways to help yourself in those moments? In my recent studies, I have found practices to accomplish just that. You can "get big", expanding your energetic structure, so that you don't feel pressured or stressed, can think clearly, and can take effective action by practicing the techniques I've described in the previous chapter, **"Basic Practices:**

---

[17] Zuckerman, Desda. *"Working at the Edge"*, private publication, 2006.

Centering, Length, Width, and Depth" and combining them with breathing practices (chapter 3, **"Notes on Breathing"**). This chapter takes those practices a step further, explaining how you can work with your extended energetic structure, based on the teachings and work of Core Individuation™ created by Desda Zuckerman. With awareness and intention, you can expand to the edge of your energetic structure: your own Edge. And when you are in a fully expanded state, circumstances, pressures and stresses that seemed overwhelming when your structure was collapsed or contracted, no longer have the same impact. You can think and move freely and have more choices available to you as a result.

The first step is to become aware of your breathing. Where is your breath located? Is it mostly high up in your chest? That's pretty normal in our fast-paced world. Take a few minutes right now to work with your breathing. Bring it down to the level of your ribs. Then down to your belly. And now use your entire torso to breath, using the full capacity of your lungs. Once you can do that, we can start to work with expanding your energetic dimensions.

REVIEW

Start by scanning through your body from top to bottom, becoming aware of your vertical alignment – your **length**. Let your breathing become narrow, moving along this vertical core. By opening to the flow of energy through your vertical core, you can touch the earth, connecting to a deep ground, while at the same time opening to spirit through the crown of your head. In many ancient teachings, we humans are seen as connectors, bringing spirit to earth and earth to spirit.

Practicing this dimension helps you stay connected to what you care about, moving in the world with inspiration while remaining "grounded" and stable.

Next, bring your breathing to your ribs. Feel your ribs moving out and expanding as you inhale, and dropping as you exhale. On the next breath, let your energy expand in the horizontal dimension, opening your **width**. This dimension is more social, and by opening yourself in the horizontal plane, you can be comfortable holding larger commitments, connect more easily with a community, feel your place in social environments, and facilitate group discussions while maintaining a connection with the individuals in the group. Let yourself open to this dimension when you feel overwhelmed, alone, despondent, or want to hold all the commitments you have made to the people you care about.

Accessing the third dimension is easier when you drop your breath to your belly. Keeping your breathing low in your torso, bring your awareness to your back, remembering all your learning, life experience, teachers, colleagues who support you, your family, friends, mentors, ancestors, and spiritual guides. Now, using focused intention, gather all that's behind you and move the energy through your torso, out in front of you, moving into your future. This is the dimension of **depth**.

When you expand your depth, you can go forward with confidence and competence, leading others toward the vision that you can hold by maintaining your vertical line and connection to what's important to you, while moving your energy forward to the horizon in front of you.

Try This:

Now for the full expansion: start by practicing full torso breathing. Begin your breath as low in your torso as you can and as you continue inhaling, feel your ribs and chest expanding as you use the full capacity of your lungs. Breathe slowly, without forcing – feel your breath filling your entire torso as you inhale, and emptying your torso as you exhale. After a few full torso breaths, expand your energy in all directions from your center, going all the way out until you sense your own outermost boundary – the **Edge** of your unique energetic structure. You might feel this Edge anywhere from five to thirty feet or more beyond your physical body. Bring your awareness out just beyond your Edge. Now settle your awareness on the outside of this Edge. Continue building your skill to maintain your awareness at your Edge. As you practice, write down your responses to the following:

- Notice how you feel in this expanded state. What can you observe now that was not available before you expanded your awareness to your Edge?

- What happens to your worries, concerns, and anxiety when you expand?

Now open your arms and send your energy out through your arms to your hands and out through your fingers. These energetic extensions from your fingers form "light fingers" that can extend all the way through your energetic structure to wrap around your Edge.

With your "light fingers" pull in a bit, bringing your Edge slightly closer to your physical body. Feel what happens as you do that. Then open your "light fingers" and let your Edge expand out further. Practice drawing your Edge in and let it out until you find a comfortable balance where you can feel your entire Structure around you, protecting you, with your awareness on your Edge. Here you are open and available, yet strong and protected. This is the optimal place for your awareness when you work. It is also optimal when you go into crowded places, or if you have a sense of being uncomfortable in any way. It really is the optimal place to be all the time. One of my clients used this practice to go through labor and delivery, saying it helped her have a focus bigger than the contractions and pain she felt when she focused only on her body. Her baby boy was able to come into the world naturally, with his mother using the practice of expanding her energetic structure with her awareness at her Edge.

- Continue practicing expanding your awareness and write down your observations and experiences as you practice.

- Note what emotional skills, communication skills, and sensory awareness become available as you continue to practice.

FOR COACHES

This is a more advanced practice, only for those students who have mastered the practices in the previous chapters. If you are confident with your own expansion, and are comfortable moving in the world while experiencing your own Edge, you may find this practice helpful for your more sensitive clients who have mastered the practices as described. As with any of the previous pieces, don't hesitate to contact me if you have any questions!

IN CONCLUSION

Thank you for working with me and experimenting with this series of distinctions and practices. I hope you are enjoying your learning, as you become more sensitive to your own body and the bodies of the people you work with, learn with, play with, dance with, and live with! If you have any questions or comments, or just want to share what you're learning by "Listening to Bodies", please let me know. You can email me at szeman@somaticbusinesscoach.com. And most importantly, have fun listening!

ACKNOWLEDGEMENTS

Bringing this book to completion has been a journey with many travelers. The road began with my teachers: Fernando Flores, who taught me to pay attention to language, for in language we create reality; Bob Dunham, who taught me management and executive skills and gave me my first coaching clients; Julio Olalla and Rafael Echeverria, who taught me the essentials for ontological coaching, brought me to California, and gave me my first coaching certification; Richard Strozzi-Heckler, who taught me to observe and work with bodies, acknowledging my innovative way of doing somatic work over the phone, inviting me to write an essay that he included in a collection of his students' work[18], and certifying me as a Master Somatic Coach; and Desda Zuckerman, who taught me about the subtle energetic body

---

[18] "Listening to Bodies Long Distance: The Power and Possibility of Telephone Coaching", Chapter 9 of Being Human At Work: Bringing Somatic Intelligence Into Your Professional Life, edited by Richard Strozzi-Heckler, North Atlantic Books, 2003.

and how to *get big*, and certified me as a practitioner of Core Individuation™.

All the students in my teleclasses called "Listening to Bodies Long Distance" have contributed to the content of this book, by engaging with me, asking clarifying questions, and applying what they learned to their work with clients and colleagues. I am so grateful to every one of you.

Without the help of my colleagues and friends who so patiently read the drafts and provided their feedback, questions and suggestions, this book would not have gotten done: Tina Maloney, Jane Perry, Will Smolak, Marcia Orlowski, Merle McKinley, Sari Broner, Leslie Warren, Tivo Rojas-Cheatham, Liz Cunningham, and Rita Dettore.

To Bob Dunham and the Company of Leaders, especially Dr. Peter Denning, Dan Waldman, Bill Maclay, Sam Ramji, and Janet Byrne-Smith, sincere gratitude for your support and care.

Thank you to Cat Weatherup for help with the cover.

And to my extraordinary friend, Andrei Marcon, who not only put up with my demands and Jersey-girl style, but willingly took on the design, production, and organization of this book – thank you from my heart.

Suzanne Zeman, MSC
a coach for coaches, executives and business teams

Somatic Business Coach
www.somaticbusinesscoach.com

phone: (510) 524-7620
fax: (510) 524-0707
szeman@comcast.net

LaVergne, TN USA
29 November 2009
165478LV00005B/225/P